Original title:
The Love Within

Copyright © 2024 Swan Charm
All rights reserved.

Author: Liina Liblikas
ISBN HARDBACK: 978-9916-89-637-2
ISBN PAPERBACK: 978-9916-89-638-9
ISBN EBOOK: 978-9916-89-639-6

Harmonies of the Heart

In twilight's glow, our hearts align,
Soft whispers drift, like aged wine.
With every note, sweet love unfolds,
A symphony that never grows old.

Beneath the stars, our dreams take flight,
In shadows deep, we find the light.
Each heartbeat sings, a tender tune,
Dancing to the rhythm of the moon.

With fingers laced, we walk the line,
Where echoes linger, pure and divine.
Through every storm, we find our way,
In harmony, forever we stay.

Caresses of the Spirit

Upon the breeze, soft touches play,
Whispers of love that gently sway.
In sacred moments, spirits blend,
A warm embrace that will not end.

With gentle hands, we weave our fate,
Each caress a dance that captivates.
In silent glances, truths are shared,
Two souls entwined, forever cared.

As dawn breaks bright, our hopes renew,
In love's embrace, we'll see it through.
With every heartbeat, we ignite,
Caresses of spirit, pure delight.

Dreamscapes of Togetherness

In starlit skies, our dreams align,
Fragments of hope in gentle sign.
With every breath, we paint the night,
In dreamscapes vast, our spirits light.

Through winding paths, we share our dreams,
In moonlit whispers, love redeems.
With laughter bright, we chase the dawn,
In togetherness, our fears are gone.

Amidst the clouds, we float and soar,
With every heartbeat, we seek more.
Together we rise, hand in hand,
In dreamscapes vast, forever we stand.

The Essence of Us

In quiet moments, we find our truth,
The essence of love, ageless youth.
With every glance, our souls converse,
In a timeless dance, a universe.

As seasons change, our bond holds tight,
In the depth of darkness, we spark light.
With every challenge that we face,
We find together, our safest place.

In laughter's echoes, in silence bold,
The essence of us, a tale retold.
Through life's vast journey, hand in hand,
Together as one, forever we stand.

A Flame That Guides

In the dark, a flicker glows,
A beacon bright, where courage flows.
It dances high, it warms the cold,
A story of the brave and bold.

With every spark, our dreams ignite,
Illuminating paths with light.
Through shadows deep, it leads the way,
A flame of hope that won't decay.

In storms that rage, it holds its ground,
A whispers soft, a guiding sound.
Though winds may blow and trials test,
This flame endures, it knows the best.

Together we shall seek the flame,
In every heart, it burns the same.
A bond of light, forever tight,
It shows the beauty in the night.

With every flicker, fears depart,
A flame that fuels the aching heart.
In unity, we find our stride,
A flame that guides, our constant pride.

Tapestry of Intimacy

Threads of laughter, woven tight,
In soft whispers, hearts take flight.
Close together, secrets shared,
In a world where love is bared.

Every glance, a story told,
Hand in hand, we break the mold.
In the fabric of each embrace,
A warmth that time cannot erase.

Colors blend, a dance of fate,
With every smile, we create.
In our tapestry, rich and grand,
A work of art, forever planned.

Fingers trace the lines we make,
In each touch, the bonds awake.
An intricate design unfolds,
A tale of warmth that never folds.

Bound by dreams, we intertwine,
In this closeness, love will shine.
A tapestry of hearts entwined,
In our embrace, peace we find.

The Quiet Pulse of Desire

Beneath the surface, whispers flow,
An echo soft, a hidden glow.
In tender depths, the heart will race,
The quiet pulse, a secret space.

Through stolen glances, sparks arise,
Each moment shared, a sweet reprise.
In silence speaks what words can't say,
Desire blooms in shades of gray.

With every heartbeat, rhythms blend,
A melody that won't just end.
In soft shadows, passion's play,
The quiet pulse guides our way.

In the hush of night, we find,
The gentle pull that stirs the mind.
A silent dance of souls in sync,
Awakening what we both think.

As fingers touch, the world dissolves,
In this moment, love resolves.
With every breath, we feel it rise,
The quiet pulse of sweet surprise.

Embracing the Invisible

The air is thick with what we crave,
An unseen force, a bond so brave.
In quiet rooms, the magic flows,
Embracing all that nobody knows.

In every heartbeat, love exists,
A gentle touch that can't be missed.
Invisible threads begin to weave,
A world so rich, we dare believe.

With every sigh, we share the air,
In simple moments, we lay bare.
The beauty found in eyes that meet,
A silent promise, soft and sweet.

In shadows where our spirits dance,
We find the strength in pure romance.
Embracing all that life conceals,
A love that flows, a truth, it reveals.

In stillness found, we come alive,
With every spark, our spirits thrive.
Embracing all that's human and real,
An invisible touch that we both feel.

Soft Serenades

Whispers under moonlit skies,
Gentle tunes that intertwine,
Hearts sway in tender sighs,
Melodies of love divine.

Stars twinkle in sweet embrace,
Notes drift through the night air,
In this quiet, sacred space,
We find solace and we care.

Each chord a story to tell,
Voices blend like softest dawn,
In dreams, we weave our spell,
Through the echoes, we're reborn.

Harmony in every glance,
Time slows beneath a sigh,
In this simple, sweet romance,
Endless is our lullaby.

So let the music play on,
Enduring like the stars above,
In every dusk, every dawn,
We live forever in love.

Glimmers of Emotion

A fleeting glance, a spark ignites,
In shadows, where hopes dare to rise,
Emotion dances through the nights,
Each heartbeat softly replies.

Colors swirl in the twilight glow,
Where laughter waits with open arms,
Glimmers of joy, a tender show,
Embracing all of our charms.

Tears may fall like gentle rain,
Yet in sorrow, strength will grow,
Through every trial, every strain,
Our spirits bright, our hearts aglow.

Time's canvas holds each fleeting dream,
Painting moments thick with light,
In the rhythm of life, we teem,
With hope as our guiding sight.

So let us cherish every hue,
For in this world, we've found our place,
With every glimmer, we renew,
The beauty wrapped in love's embrace.

The Sanctuary of Us

In a world so vast and wide,
We built a space that feels like home,
With every glance, we turn the tide,
In our hearts, no need to roam.

Laughter dances in the air,
As shadows play on walls of trust,
In this haven, love lays bare,
A refuge built on hope and lust.

We carve our names in fleeting time,
With dreams that twinkle in our eyes,
The rhythm of our hearts, a rhyme,
Together under endless skies.

Soft whispers weave through night's embrace,
As silence cradles every word,
In this sanctuary, our grace,
In every moment, love is stirred.

So here we stay, forever near,
A fortress strong, where dreams align,
In the sanctuary we hold dear,
Two souls entwined, forever shine.

Silence Speaks

In quiet corners, secrets dwell,
Where whispers fade into the night,
In silence, stories weave and swell,
A tapestry of inner light.

The absence of sound can sing,
A language all its own,
In gentle pauses, feelings spring,
A sacred hush, not overthrown.

With every breath, a promise made,
In stillness, lives intertwine,
Through every shadow, fears allayed,
In silence, hearts begin to shine.

Moments stretch like endless time,
Where hearts converse without a word,
In every stillness, love will climb,
A language felt but never heard.

So let us dance in silent grace,
In the spaces where we belong,
For in this calm, we find our place,
In silence speaks our deepest song.

Oaths in Shadows

In the dark, we make our pact,
Silhouettes dance, a silent act.
Words like whispers, soft and low,
Promises forged where few dare go.

With every gaze, the shadows creep,
Secrets whispered, vows we keep.
Silent witnesses, the night holds tight,
Our boundless love outshines the light.

Through the veil, our hearts align,
In uncharted realms, our spirits intertwine.
Oaths exchanged, beneath the moon,
A melody played, the perfect tune.

Each heartbeat echoes a cherished dream,
Trust and loyalty, a radiant beam.
In shadows cast, no fear remains,
Together we dance through joy and pains.

From dusk to dawn, we stand as one,
In the quiet dusk, our lives begun.
Oaths in shadows, forever bound,
In silent strength, true love is found.

Whispers of Forever

In the soft breeze, your name I hear,
Whispers of forever, drawing near.
Promises float on gentle sighs,
Eternal love beneath moonlit skies.

Every heartbeat a soothing song,
In your embrace, where I belong.
Gentle echoes of dreams we share,
Together we rise, a perfect pair.

As dawn breaks, the world awakes,
In warm light, our spirit shakes.
With every step, a path unfolds,
In whispers of forever, love it holds.

Time may falter, seasons change,
Yet our hearts remain unstrange.
In silent moments, we silently vow,
To cherish the now, the sacred how.

Together we tread the winding road,
In every challenge, love's true code.
In whispers of forever, we will find,
A bond unbroken, forever entwined.

Warmth in Winter

Beneath the frost, the world sleeps tight,
Yet in our hearts, there's burning light.
Crackling fires and smiles so bright,
Together we find our pure delight.

Wrapped in blankets, we share tales,
Of distant shores and gentle gales.
In every glance, a spark ignites,
Warmth in winter, our love invites.

Outside, the chill may bite and gnash,
But in our haven, spirits clash.
Each laughter shared, a flickering flame,
In cozy moments, we stake our claim.

Through swirling snow, a path we tread,
With every step, nothing to dread.
In frozen times, our hearts entwine,
Warmth in winter, a love divine.

As seasons shift, and winters fade,
The warmth we forged won't be betrayed.
In every memory, we shall find,
Eternal warmth, forever kind.

Secrets Under the Stars

In the night, whispers low,
Dreams take flight, hearts aglow.
Shadows dance, secrets sigh,
Underneath the vast, dark sky.

Old tales spin, stories weave,
Magic found in what we believe.
Stars align in silent grace,
Holding time in their embrace.

Hope flickers, twinkles bright,
Guiding souls through endless night.
Each moment, a precious gift,
In the stars, our spirits lift.

Wishes cast, softly spoken,
Promises made, never broken.
Together we roam, hand in hand,
In this twilight wonderland.

Echoes linger, love's refrain,
Beneath the moon, no pain.
In the night, we find our way,
With secrets shared till break of day.

The Canvas of Us

Brushes dipped in hues divine,
Each stroke tells our story line.
Colors blend, a dance so sweet,
On this canvas, hearts do meet.

Whispers of laughter, silence too,
Every shade speaks of me and you.
Masterpiece formed through time's embrace,
Captured moments that we trace.

In splashes bright of joy and pain,
Together we rise, together we gain.
Each layer shows the bond we mold,
A tapestry of love untold.

From past to present, futures lean,
In every shadow, a light is seen.
Artistry born from deep inside,
Where our souls forever bide.

As seasons change, the colors shift,
Yet in our hearts, the flame's a gift.
On this canvas, our lives entwine,
An endless portrait, you are mine.

Melodies of Us

Softly strummed, the strings resound,
In our heartbeats, love is found.
Rhythms pulse, dancing free,
In this song, it's you and me.

Lyrics penned in whispered dreams,
Harmony flows in silver beams.
Each note a step, a breath, a sigh,
Together we soar, you and I.

Chords entwined, a perfect blend,
Timeless echoes that never end.
Every laugh, each shared embrace,
Compose the music, our sacred space.

In the silence, still we sing,
Every heartstring gently clinging.
Melodies weave, our spirits fly,
In the symphony of the sky.

As the world turns, our song remains,
In every joy, in every pain.
Forever bound in sweet refrain,
Together's where we'll always reign.

Fusion of Spirits

In the twilight, spirits merge,
Hearts aligned, we feel the surge.
Dancing flames, a vibrant glow,
In this moment, love will flow.

Two souls intertwine like vines,
In soft whispers, our world shines.
Boundless energy, passion ignites,
Together we brew, stars and lights.

Unity found in gentle grace,
In your eyes, my sacred place.
Every heartbeat a cosmic thread,
In this fusion, fears are shed.

Here we stand, a force so rare,
Through joy and sorrow, always there.
Spirits strong, we cannot break,
In love's embrace, we both awake.

As day breaks, our fire glows,
In every breath, our spirit flows.
Together we rise, a sunrise spark,
In this dance, we leave our mark.

The Embrace of Eternity

In the depths of night we dwell,
Time suspends its gentle spell.
Stars align in silent gleam,
Together we weave a dream.

Moments stretch into the vast,
Holding tight to memories cast.
Every heartbeat sings our song,
In this space where we belong.

Infinity wraps us in light,
Guiding souls through endless flight.
With each whisper, shadows fade,
In love's warmth, we're unafraid.

As the dawn embraces night,
Hope ignites the morning bright.
In this embrace, we find the key,
Unraveling eternity.

Time may wane and seasons change,
Yet our bond will not derange.
In the cosmos, ever free,
Together, you and me.

Threads of Affinity

In the fabric of the night,
We are woven, pure and right.
Each thread binds our story tight,
Colors dance in shared delight.

Silken whispers in the breeze,
Carrying souls with such ease.
Gossamer dreams softly interlace,
Bringing kindred hearts to grace.

Amongst the stars, patterns shine,
Every thread a tale divine.
With every stitch, a bond we sew,
In the loom where passions flow.

Entwined destinies unite,
Gentle shadows hold us tight.
In the tapestry of fate,
Love's design we celebrate.

Together we create and play,
In this vibrant, radiant way.
Threads of affinity, bright and true,
Binding me forever to you.

Whispers of the Heart

In the silence, love awakes,
Sweetest secrets, softly breaks.
Whispers linger on the air,
Tender moments laid bare.

Quiet gazes, souls entwined,
In your eyes, my heart aligned.
Every sigh, a story told,
In your warmth, I find my hold.

Gentle echoes fill the night,
Carrying our purest light.
With each heartbeat, dreams ignite,
Together, we take flight.

The world fades, just you and me,
In this hush, our spirits free.
Whispers weaving through the dark,
Unveiling love's eternal spark.

When dawn breaks, the silence fades,
Yet in our hearts, the echo stays.
Whispers linger, ever sweet,
In this journey, love's heartbeat.

In the Shade of Us

Underneath the willow's sway,
In the shade, we find our way.
Softest whispers, laughter shared,
In this haven, we are spared.

Leaves above us twirl and glide,
In this calm, our hearts confide.
Moments wrapped in soft embrace,
Time stands still in this sacred space.

Sunbeams filter through the green,
Painting dreams in patterns seen.
In the shade, our worries cease,
Here, we find a world of peace.

Gentle breezes carry tunes,
Harmonizing with the moons.
In this bond, our spirits fuse,
In the shade of me and you.

Seasons change, yet love stays true,
In the shade, we start anew.
Underneath the sky so vast,
Together, we can outlast.

Unfurling Hearts

In twilight's gentle embrace we meet,
Soft whispers dance on the evening air.
Petals unfolding in the softest heat,
Hearts unfurl slowly, stripped of care.

Stars above us twinkle and gleam,
Painting dreams on canvas of night.
With every sigh, we weave a dream,
In this silence, all feels just right.

Your laughter blooms like flowers in spring,
Coloring shadows with joyous light.
In shared moments, our spirits sing,
Guided by love, we take flight.

Let the world around us fade away,
As we lose ourselves in this trance.
Together we'll navigate the sway,
In our hearts, we find the dance.

Softly we promise, come what may,
With each heartbeat, we'll draw near.
With every sunset, we'll find our way,
Unfurling love, pure and sincere.

Tidal Waves of Affection

The ocean breathes a balmy sigh,
Waves crashing gently on the shore.
With every tide, my heart will fly,
As your love calls, I crave more.

Swirling currents, deep and wide,
Emotions rise like the ocean spray.
In your embrace, I want to glide,
Tidal waves of affection sway.

Silver moonlight guides the night,
Casting shadows where we stand.
In this moment, everything's right,
As we walk together, hand in hand.

Seashell secrets whispered in hush,
Every echo carries your name.
With the soft pulse of nature's rush,
Our souls ignite in love's sweet flame.

Let the storms brew, let winds roar,
Our bond is a fortress, strong and true.
Tidal waves will crash to the shore,
But I'll always return to you.

Garden of Affection

In a garden where memories bloom,
Petals unfold beneath the sun.
With every heartbeat, dispel the gloom,
Two souls entwined, forever one.

Nurtured by laughter, watered with care,
Every flower tells our sweet tale.
In the fragrant air, love lingers there,
Together we grow, we shall not fail.

Butterflies dance in playful flight,
Painting colors on a canvas bright.
Within this space, our dreams ignite,
In a garden of love, pure delight.

Seasons shift, yet we remain,
Rooted in trust, through joy and pain.
As the world changes, we bear the strain,
In this garden, we'll thrive again.

With every sunrise, new blooms shall rise,
A testament to the love we sow.
In this sanctuary where hope lies,
Our garden flourishes, forever to grow.

Ties of Kindred Spirit

Beneath the stars, our spirits gleam,
A connection deeper than the sea.
In every glance, I find my dream,
Ties of kindred spirit, you and me.

Each laughter shared paints the night,
With colors rich and stories old.
In your presence, wrong feels right,
A bond that's warm, a treasure untold.

Through every storm and gentle breeze,
We journey forward, side by side.
In quiet moments, the heart feels ease,
With every step, love is our guide.

Hand in hand, we face the dawn,
Discovering joy in all we find.
With passion's fire, and fears long gone,
These ties will only further bind.

In the tapestry of life, we weave,
Threads of memories, bright and clear.
Together always, we shall believe,
In kindred spirits, forever near.

Emotive Resonance

In whispers soft, the heart does speak,
Echoes linger, emotions peak.
A tidal wave of joy and pain,
In shadows cast, love's sweet refrain.

Memories linger, fragile and bright,
Dancing dreams in the silent night.
With every tear, the soul unfolds,
A tapestry of stories told.

The laughter shared, the sorrow embraced,
Each moment etched, time can't erase.
In every heartbeat, a symphony,
Resonating through you and me.

In fleeting glances, our worlds collide,
Moments captured, no need to hide.
A sigh, a smile, a lingering glance,
Within our hearts, a timeless dance.

Emotive storms, where passions play,
Unraveling truth in shades of gray.
Together, we rise, apart we fall,
In this embrace, we find it all.

Shades of Unity

In colors bold, we intertwine,
Each hue a story, yours and mine.
In every shade, a common thread,
Bringing forth what once was said.

From dawn to dusk, together we stand,
In harmony, hand in hand.
The rich palette of our shared fate,
In unity, we learn to create.

Different voices, yet one song,
A melody where we belong.
In every note, the echo clear,
Boundless love in every tear.

With every heartbeat, we align,
Finding strength in what's divine.
In moments small, in actions grand,
Together, we rise, hand in hand.

Across the spectrum, we will grow,
In perfect sync, the world will know.
Every whisper, every shout,
In shades of unity, we work it out.

Dancing in Quietude

In gentle stillness, we take flight,
Beneath the stars, wrapped in twilight.
The world outside begins to fade,
In this soft space, dreams are laid.

With whispered moves, the night unfolds,
Stories woven in silence told.
As shadows swirl, we lose our way,
In quietude, we laugh and sway.

A dance of hearts, a breath divine,
Lost in rhythm, your hand in mine.
With every pause, the silence sings,
In this embrace, the stillness swings.

In whispers soft and echoes near,
The dance returns, dissolving fear.
With every step, we find our grace,
In quietude, our sacred space.

A symphony of tranquil night,
In every glance, our souls ignite.
Together swaying, time stands still,
In this embrace, our hearts we fill.

Interlaced Journeys

Two paths converge, a fateful spin,
In every twist, where dreams begin.
With open hearts, we step in time,
Our journeys weave, a tale sublime.

Through winding roads, we laugh and cry,
In each encounter, we learn to fly.
The stories shared, the moments bright,
Together we chase the fading light.

From mountains high to rivers wide,
In every journey, you've been my guide.
With every challenge, we face the day,
In interlaced journeys, we find our way.

Through storms and sun, our spirits soar,
In every chapter, we yearn for more.
In laughter's echo and love's embrace,
We map our dreams in this endless space.

Each twist and turn, a chance to grow,
With every smile, the love will flow.
Interlaced journeys, hand in hand,
Together we walk, together we stand.

Heartstrings in Harmony

In this dance of light and shade,
We find our hearts unafraid.
Each note a whisper, soft and clear,
Binding us close, forever near.

Hands entwined, we sway and spin,
Where love begins, and strife grows thin.
A melody that we compose,
In tender beats, our passion flows.

Through storms and calm, we ride the waves,
In harmony, each truth we save.
The world may change, but here we stay,
Singing sweet songs, come what may.

In twilight's glow, we share a sigh,
Our heartstrings pull beneath the sky.
Together, we are strong and bold,
A story woven, love retold.

As seasons pass, our symphony,
Grows richer still, in perfect key.
In every heartbeat, every glance,
We write our love, a timeless dance.

The Fabric of Togetherness

Woven threads of laughter, cheer,
In every stitch, we hold what's dear.
A tapestry of joy and grace,
Each moment shared, our special place.

Layered colors, bright and warm,
Through trials faced, we find our form.
United hearts, we weave as one,
In harmony, our journey's spun.

With every tear, we stitch anew,
A fabric strong, in shades of blue.
Through winters cold and summers bright,
Our woven bond is pure delight.

As seasons shift, we change our hue,
Yet never lose the love that's true.
Each thread a story, bold and vast,
Together, we will always last.

In the quiet, we find our strength,
In every distance, every length.
A patchwork quilt, we find our peace,
In the fabric of love, we find release.

Unchartered Affection

In whispers soft, our hearts confide,
Through uncharted paths, we choose to glide.
No map in hand, yet still we roam,
In love's embrace, we find our home.

With every step, new dreams arise,
In gentle glances, wonder lies.
Exploring depths both wide and deep,
A treasure found, our love to keep.

Through twilight's veil and dawn's first light,
We chase the stars, ignite the night.
Together, we unveil the thrill,
Of uncharted love that time can't fill.

With hands outstretched, we brave the new,
In moments shared, our spirits grew.
Each heartbeat echoes, wild and free,
In our adventure, just you and me.

In this vast world, we carve our way,
An odyssey where hearts can play.
Through uncharted lands, our love will soar,
Forever seeking, forever more.

Shadow Play of Souls

In the quiet dusk, shadows dance,
A ballet formed in love's romance.
With every step, we spin and sway,
In the twilight's soft embrace, we play.

Our shadows merge, a gentle blend,
Two souls entwined, a timeless trend.
With every gaze, each tender sigh,
In shadow play, we learn to fly.

Unspoken dreams in quiet night,
Illuminate our hearts with light.
In the stillness, we find our way,
Lost in the echo of yesterday.

Hand in hand, we chase the light,
Transforming fear into pure flight.
In shadows cast, our spirits soar,
Forging a bond forevermore.

With every whisper, sparks ignite,
A symphony of dark and light.
In the dance of our souls, we find,
The beauty woven in the blind.

Threads of Connection

In the tapestry of lives entwined,
We find solace in shared breaths.
Silken threads of laughter combine,
Creating bonds that outlast death.

Through storms and trials, we stand tall,
Each whisper carries a warm light.
In the silence, we hear the call,
A heartbeat echoing the night.

Like stars that shine in the dark sky,
We navigate this vast unknown.
When you stumble, I'm nearby,
In every struggle, you're not alone.

With every message, every sign,
An invisible string draws us near.
In moments quiet, love will shine,
In our hearts, there's nothing to fear.

Together we weave our story bright,
With colors of joy, sorrow, and grace.
In this dance, our spirits take flight,
Forever connected, we find our place.

Infinite Emotions

In the spectrum of a heart's swell,
A myriad feelings take shape.
From soft whispers to loud bell,
Each moment's hue decides our fate.

Like waves that crash upon the shore,
Joy rises, then fades into tears.
In laughter, we always want more,
In silence, we face our deep fears.

Through the lens of love we see,
The beauty in moments mundane.
In every heartbeat, we agree,
Life's dance is a sweet refrain.

With every glance, the world expands,
Colors blend in vast waves of light.
Feelings weave like gentle hands,
Guiding us through the endless night.

In the end, we learn to embrace,
Each emotion, a thread in our tale.
Together, we journey's warm grace,
In infinite circles, we sail.

Gentle Embrace

In the quiet of evening's glow,
A soft touch lingers on skin.
With arms wrapped tight, worries flow,
In warmth, a new journey begins.

The heartbeat echoes in time's dance,
Two souls lost in the tender space.
In shared silence, we find romance,
A haven where we both find grace.

With every sigh, we melt like snow,
As moments whisper through the night.
In this cocoon, our spirits grow,
Bathing in love's gentle light.

Each embrace holds a world apart,
A refuge from time's swift command.
In that warmth, there's peace to impart,
In the solace of a close hand.

Through the storms, we find our way,
In gentle embraces, we trust.
For love's warmth will always stay,
In the ashes of dreams we must.

Blossoms in the Heart

Like spring blooms breaking through the frost,
Hope emerges in each new day.
In the garden where dreams are tossed,
Petals weave a vibrant display.

With each smile, a flower blooms,
Coloring spaces once barren.
In laughter, the bouquet assumes,
A fragrance sweet, bright and clarion.

Together we witness the growth,
Roots intertwining deep beneath.
In unity, we make our oath,
To nurture love, warmth, and peace.

Though seasons change and winds can howl,
We stand firm in life's grand array.
In our hearts' garden, we'll take a vow,
To cherish each petal come what may.

For in this sacred, tender place,
Blossoms teach us how to be.
With each heartbeat, we trace,
A love that's as vast as the sea.

Tunnels of Togetherness

In shadows where whispers dwell,
We weave our stories, silent spell.
Hand in hand, we breathe the night,
Tunnels carved in shared delight.

Through darkness, the light does break,
Together, we rise, no fear to shake.
Voices echo in the deep,
A bond so strong, forever keep.

Each step resonates with grace,
In the warmth of a familiar space.
Tunnels bend, yet never break,
Together, all the risks we take.

In laughter's glow, together we stand,
A journey drawn in heart and hand.
With every turn, our spirits blend,
The path is ours, a means to mend.

Time may twist, but love will guide,
In tunnels where our dreams reside.
With every heartbeat, we define,
The strength of souls, forever twine.

The Stream of Connection

A river flows with gentle grace,
Reflecting light, our sacred space.
Each ripple tells a tale so true,
In currents deep, I find you too.

We gather stones, each one a thought,
In the stream where love is sought.
Through bends and turns, we find the way,
To cherish moments, come what may.

Whispers ride on water's breath,
A dance that edges near to death.
Yet in this stream, we laugh and cry,
Holding memories as we fly.

The flow unites, no end in sight,
Our spirits soar, taking flight.
A bond in motion, fresh and free,
In the stream, just you and me.

Through quiet nights and sunny days,
Our hearts entwined in nature's ways.
With every wave, we drift, we steer,
The stream of life brings us near.

A Pulse of Two

In sync, our hearts begin to beat,
A rhythm strong, a song so sweet.
Within each pulse, the world fades out,
In sounds of love, we scream and shout.

The dance of souls, a vibrant hue,
Our every breath, a spark brand new.
Together in this sacred space,
We find our home, a warm embrace.

Through stormy nights and skies of blue,
The pulse remains, steadfast and true.
In every moment, love's refrain,
We share the joy, the grief, the pain.

Like echoes in the vast expanse,
Our hearts engage in timeless dance.
A pulse of two, forever shared,
In life's great fabric, we are paired.

With every beat, a vow we take,
To stand as one, for love's own sake.
Together strong, we'll brave the tide,
In every pulse, we will abide.

Glimmers of Belonging

In twilight shade, our spirits glow,
A tapestry of love we sew.
Glimmers shine through clouds of gray,
In every word, we find our way.

Like stars that dot the velvet sky,
We seek connection, you and I.
With every laugh and shared embrace,
We carve our niche, our sacred place.

Together, facing what may come,
In every heart, a steady drum.
Glimmers speak of bonds so rare,
In moments shared, we show we care.

With open hearts, we capture light,
In shadows deep, we spark the night.
Glimmers glint, a guiding sign,
In the web of life, you are mine.

In every whisper, trust takes flight,
In glimmers found, we share our light.
Hand in hand, our journey long,
In the symphony of us, we belong.

Dance of Hearts

In shadows soft, we twirl and sway,
Unspoken rhythm guides our way.
With whispered dreams that intertwine,
Our souls ignite, your heart with mine.

Notes of laughter fill the air,
Each step a promise, light as air.
In this embrace, the world dissolves,
As in our dance, the silence evolves.

Through every spin, a secret shared,
In every glance, a spark declared.
The beat of love, it knows no end,
Together in this dance, we blend.

We move in circles, time eludes,
In outer worlds, our hearts exclude.
The universe in every sound,
In perfect sync, our love is found.

As night descends and stars appear,
In twilight's glow, your face shines clear.
With every dip, our spirits soar,
In this dance, we ask for more.

Intimate Horizons

Upon the cliffs where shadows lie,
We share our dreams, the earth, the sky.
With whispered hopes, our fingers trace,
The intimate line of time and space.

The sun dips low, a golden hue,
In every glance, I see the true.
Together, we paint horizons wide,
In silent vows, where hearts confide.

The world dissolves, it fades from sight,
In shared secrets, we find our light.
Our laughter mingles with the breeze,
In gentle moments, we find our ease.

With every heartbeat, time stands still,
In every word, a longing thrill.
The stars emerge, a canvas bright,
In this embrace, we find our flight.

The night unfolds, we dream as one,
In intimate spaces, we've just begun.
A tapestry of wishes spun,
In this horizon, love has won.

Harmony in Silence

In quiet spaces, hearts align,
Where words unspoken intertwine.
The stillness hums a tender tune,
In harmony beneath the moon.

With every breath, the world retreats,
In silence, our own heartbeat meets.
A glance, a touch, no need for sound,
In tranquil love, our souls are bound.

The stars above, a witness true,
To every moment shared by two.
In gentle whispers, closeness grows,
As nature blooms, our story flows.

Through hidden realms, our spirits roam,
In silent echoes, we've found home.
Within the calm, our fears release,
In harmony, we find our peace.

While life may rush, we choose to stay,
In quietude, we find our way.
Together, wrapped in soft embrace,
In silent love, we find our place.

Shared Breath

In the spaces where we linger close,
With every sigh, our hearts engross.
A shared breath, a fleeting pause,
In love's embrace, we find our cause.

With gentle winds, our spirits soar,
In whispered dreams, we seek for more.
Every moment, an ocean wide,
Two souls united, side by side.

In tender touch, the world dissolves,
In every gaze, our truth evolves.
We weave our time, a fragile thread,
In shared breath, our lives are led.

As twilight dances in the air,
In every heartbeat, love declared.
With every pulse, a promise made,
In this connection, fears must fade.

Together we rise, no fear of night,
In shared breath, we find our light.
As dawn approaches, hearts still blend,
In this sweet circle, love transcends.

Veils of Affection

In soft shadows, love resides,
Gentle whispers, no need to hide.
Wrapped in warmth, moments divine,
Two souls dance, your heart in mine.

Each caress, a tender bond,
In silence, our hearts respond.
Veils of trust, gently unfold,
Stories of warmth, quietly told.

Fingers trace the lightest way,
In the evening, where dreams play.
A fragile touch, a fleeting spark,
Together we illuminate the dark.

Beneath the stars, our wishes blend,
In every sigh, beginnings mend.
Every heartbeat, a silent vow,
In veils of affection, we live now.

Transcendental Caresses

In the ether, soft and light,
Fingers dance, igniting night.
Transcendental whispers flow,
Each caress, a subtle glow.

Moments drift on velvet breeze,
Time is still, the world at ease.
In your arms, love's sweetest grace,
A fleeting breath, our secret place.

Thoughts entwined like ivy's climb,
Through the shadows, hearts align.
Bright horizons pull us near,
In your gaze, I lose my fear.

Waves of warmth, cascading light,
Carry dreams beyond the night.
Transcendent touch, a soft embrace,
In every heartbeat, we find grace.

Stolen Glances

In crowded rooms, our eyes collide,
Unspoken words that can't abide.
Stolen glances, quick and shy,
In your gaze, the reasons lie.

A fleeting smile, a moment's pause,
Time suspends for a silent cause.
The world fades, just you and me,
In stolen glances, we are free.

Underneath the moon's embrace,
Secret worlds in every space.
Every look, a tender theft,
In the silence, love is left.

Passions spark in hidden sighs,
Language lost in soft replies.
In the shadows, hearts advance,
We discover love's sweet dance.

Whispers of Forever

In twilight's glow, dreams take flight,
Whispers weave through the night.
Eternal love, beyond the road,
In gentle murmurs, the truth is showed.

Stars align in tender grace,
In each heartbeat, I find my place.
Whispers of forever ignite,
In your arms, everything feels right.

Promises flow like rivers wide,
With each glance, there's no need to hide.
In the silence, we both confide,
Through time and space, love's boundless tide.

Each moment lingers, sweet and rare,
With every breath, I choose to care.
Conversations laced in hope's delight,
Whispers of forever in the night.

Hearts Intertwined

In the quiet of the night, we meet,
Whispers dance on hearts discreet.
Two souls merge like flowing streams,
In a tapestry of tender dreams.

Your laughter, a melody in the air,
Pulls me close, erasing care.
Hand in hand, we stroll through time,
Fingers laced, our rhythms rhyme.

Each glance a spark, igniting flame,
In a world that feels so tame.
Together we paint the canvas bright,
With hues of love and pure delight.

Moments precious, wrapped in grace,
In your eyes, I find my place.
With every heartbeat, we align,
In this dance, our hearts entwined.

Seasons change, yet we remain,
Bound by love, free from pain.
In the stars, our dreams take flight,
Forever shining, day and night.

Whispered Affections

Beneath the moon's soft silver glow,
Gentle whispers begin to flow.
Every word, a love letter spun,
Binding hearts, two become one.

Silent promises in the night,
Chasing shadows, seeking light.
With each secret shared so sweet,
Our connection grows, bittersweet.

Soft caresses and tender sighs,
A world within each other's eyes.
In close embraces, time stands still,
As soft echoes of love fulfill.

You and I, a timeless tale,
Sailing on love's endless gale.
With every heartbeat, we draw near,
Whispered affections, loud and clear.

Through the storms and calm we face,
We find solace in our space.
In every moment, sweet and rare,
Whispers linger, filling the air.

Echoes of Soft Embrace

In the dawn where light breaks free,
I find comfort alongside thee.
Like a gentle breeze, your touch remains,
Echoing through my heart's domains.

With every sigh, the world fades away,
In your arms, I long to stay.
Moments unfold like petals at dawn,
In this warmth, I feel reborn.

Laughter dances, echoing wide,
In this refuge, we confide.
Each memory, a stepping stone,
In the tapestry we have sewn.

Your voice, a song that fills the air,
In every note, a tender care.
Wrapped in love, we softly sway,
Echoes of embrace leading the way.

In twilight's glow, we linger still,
Two hearts united, time to fill.
As shadows stretch and softly chase,
We are one in this warm embrace.

Threads of Connection

In the weave of fate's design,
I find threads that intertwine.
Binding us in a sacred dance,
Creating paths with each glance.

With gentle hands, we pull so tight,
Crafting dreams that feel so right.
In the fabric of our shared days,
Connection blooms in myriad ways.

Like a quilt pieced with care and love,
Every stitch, a push and shove.
Holding us in moments rare,
Threads of connection, bright and fair.

Through trials faced and joys embraced,
In every heartbeat, love is traced.
Together, in this grand design,
We find our stories, purely divine.

In the silence, our souls converse,
Bound by love, we share a verse.
In every fiber, we confess,
Threads of connection, nothing less.

Radiance of Companionship

In laughter's glow we find our way,
Through shadowed paths, we choose to stay.
A bond of light that warms the soul,
Together we make each other whole.

In silence shared, our hearts align,
Each whispered thought, a thread divine.
With every glance, the world feels right,
Companionship, our guiding light.

We wander fields where wildflowers bloom,
In every moment, dispelling gloom.
With hands entwined, we face the storm,
In friendship's fire, we grow warm.

Through seasons change, our roots go deep,
The promise of love, a vow we keep.
In every heartbeat, a story spun,
Radiance blooms where two become one.

As day gives way to tranquil night,
We find our dreams take gentle flight.
In the starry sky, our wishes dance,
Together we embrace this chance.

Echoes of Intimacy

In quiet corners, whispers dwell,
Where secrets linger, hearts can tell.
A gaze that speaks of hidden dreams,
In intimate trust, love softly gleams.

We share our fears, our hopes, our tears,
In the tender silence, the heart clears.
With every touch, the world recedes,
Echoes of love plant gentle seeds.

Forgotten spaces turn to hazes,
Moments cherished through time's phases.
With every heartbeat, our bond does grow,
In intimacy's warmth, we ebb and flow.

In the gentle night, where shadows lie,
We share our laughter, hear each sigh.
The quiet moments, so truly grand,
Together we walk, hand in hand.

A sanctuary found in soft embrace,
In every heartbeat, a sacred place.
Through whispered words and stolen glances,
Echoes of intimacy give life to chances.

Ties Untold

In unseen bonds, our stories weave,
Through trials shared, we learn to believe.
A connection deep, wrapped in trust,
In the fabric of life, we find our must.

The laughter and tears, a tapestry bright,
Through tangled paths, we find the light.
With every moment, our hearts grow bold,
In the warmth of memories, ties unfold.

Roots intertwined beneath the ground,
In the quiet whispers, love is found.
From every struggle, a lesson learned,
In the ties untold, the passion burned.

Together we rise, through thick and thin,
In the dance of life, we both shall spin.
A journey vast where we both belong,
In the bonds of love, we grow strong.

And as the seasons gently change,
Each tie we've forged, unique and strange.
In unity, we write our fate,
Ties untold resonate, never late.

Sanctuary of Affection

In the quiet spaces, love takes flight,
A sanctuary built in soft sunlight.
With open hearts, we find our home,
In affection's warmth, we freely roam.

Through laughter shared and gentle sighs,
In tender glances, the spirit flies.
Each heartbeat echoes in sweet refrain,
A refuge found from joy and pain.

As waves of comfort wash ashore,
In love's embrace, we long for more.
With every word, a bond we build,
In the sanctuary, our hearts fulfilled.

Together we weave a shelter vast,
A place where shadows cannot cast.
In the cradle of dreams, we find our peace,
In the sanctuary of love, we seek release.

Through every storm, our shelter stands,
In the warmth of love, we hold hands.
With every dawn, new hopes arise,
Sanctuary of affection, forever ties.

Heartfelt Serenade

In twilight's glow, we speak in sighs,
With whispered dreams that softly rise.
Your laughter dances in the air,
A melody, beyond compare.

The stars align, our wishes shared,
In every glance, a love declared.
With gentle hands, we trace the night,
Two hearts as one, a pure delight.

Through every storm, we find our way,
In shadows deep, a brighter day.
Your presence warms my fleeting thoughts,
In every breath, my solace caught.

As moonlight weaves our timeless tale,
Together, love will never pale.
Each note we play, a sweet refrain,
In every song, I feel your pain.

With every beat, our spirits soar,
In harmony, we'll seek for more.
A heartfelt serenade we sing,
In tune with joy that love can bring.

Tides of Emotion

The ocean waves, they ebb and flow,
Like feelings deep, they rise and go.
In salty air, our secrets blend,
A shoreline love that knows no end.

Beneath the stars, our dreams take flight,
In every tide, a shared delight.
With every wave, my heart does race,
In your embrace, I find my place.

The whispers of the sea do call,
They carry hopes, they rise and fall.
Through every storm, through every calm,
Your presence brings a soothing balm.

As moonbeams kiss the water's face,
We dance in time, a gentle pace.
The tides of love will pull us near,
In every swell, I hold you dear.

Light of Togetherness

In candle's glow, our shadows dance,
Each flicker sparks a sweet romance.
The warmth of love, a guiding flame,
In radiant light, we're never same.

With every step, we share the glow,
In every laugh, our spirits flow.
A beacon bright, through darkened nights,
Your smile shines, a world of lights.

Together, we will face the dawn,
As trails of gold lead us along.
In every moment, hand in hand,
We'll build a life, a promised land.

In harmony, our hearts entwined,
With every breath, our love defined.
A light that guides, forever stays,
In the warmth of together days.

Unseen Currents

Beneath the surface, rivers flow,
With unseen force, they twist and grow.
In silent depths, our feelings hide,
Yet pull us closer, side by side.

Invisible threads that tie us tight,
In moments dark, they guide our flight.
A current strong, unseen yet clear,
Through every challenge, love draws near.

The ebb and flow of life we chase,
With whispered hopes in a hidden space.
With every turn, our souls do leap,
In currents deep, our dreams do seep.

Though tides may shift, we find our way,
In currents strong, come what may.
Our love, a force that cannot fade,
In unseen currents, we are made.

The Symphony of Us

In the quiet of dusk's embrace,
Our laughter dances, leaves a trace.
Melodies weave through the air,
Moments captured, beyond compare.

Every glance, a note sublime,
Together, we beat the hands of time.
In harmony, our hearts will blend,
A symphony that won't descend.

Through storms and sunny skies we soar,
A chorus that forever explores.
With every dream, we sing our song,
Together, where we both belong.

In twilight's glow we trace our fate,
In sync, we move, we resonate.
A serenade beneath the stars,
Our rhythms echo near and far.

For in this song, we'll always find,
The essence of our intertwined.
An artful dance, both bold and true,
A symphony shaped from me and you.

Threads of Belonging

In the fabric of our days entwined,
We stitch the moments, pure and kind.
Each thread a tale, a gentle bond,
Together here, of love we're fond.

We weave through laughter and through tears,
Strengthened by all our shared years.
Patterns formed by every choice,
In the loom of life, we find our voice.

With every stitch, a memory made,
In colors bright, our fears allayed.
A tapestry of joy and strife,
Threads of belonging, woven life.

Through seasons change, we hold it tight,
In every shade, a spark of light.
Bound together, hearts in sync,
In the fabric of love, we never blink.

So let us craft, with patient hands,
A heritage that forever stands.
In every loop, the story's spun,
Threads of belonging, forever one.

Evening Strolls

We wander softly, hand in hand,
Through quiet streets, across the land.
The sun dips low, the skies ablaze,
In every step, we find our gaze.

With whispers low, we share our dreams,
As shadows dance by silver beams.
The world a canvas, painted bright,
In every heart, a spark of light.

Crisp air wraps 'round with a gentle touch,
In those sweet moments, we feel so much.
The evening calls with a soft refrain,
In stillness found, our spirits gain.

Footsteps echo on cobblestone,
Each memory made, we're never alone.
Beneath the stars, we pause and breathe,
In this life's stroll, our hearts believe.

With every smile, a story we tell,
On evening strolls, all is well.
As moonlight guides us, hand in hand,
In this embrace, we understand.

Harmonious Paths

Two souls converge on winding trails,
Each step resounds, a story sails.
With nature's hymn, our hearts align,
In every breath, the world feels fine.

Amidst the trees, our laughter rings,
In harmony, our spirit sings.
Each curve we take, a dance of fate,
Together we move, never late.

As sunlight filters through the leaves,
In this embrace, our spirit weaves.
With vibrant hues, our journey goes,
On paths unknown, our love still grows.

With every step, a rhythm found,
In silence shared, our hearts resound.
Through life's great symphony, we stride,
Harmonious paths, side by side.

In twilight's glow, the day will end,
Together still, our hearts extend.
As stars appear, we find our way,
In harmonious paths, forever stay.

The Space Between

In twilight's hush, we softly speak,
Words float like whispers, gentle, meek.
In the shadows, dreams take flight,
Bridging the space, from day to night.

Stars shimmer softly, a guiding light,
Echoes of laughter, stars burning bright.
Hands reach across, the void we mend,
In the silence, love's ways transcend.

Waves tug at shores, a timeless dance,
Moments exchanged, a fleeting glance.
Time may divide, but heartbeats align,
In the space between, our souls entwine.

Fleeting like shadows, yet steadfast, true,
In every heartbeat, I find you.
Though miles apart, we always align,
In the space between, your heart is mine.

A tapestry woven, thread by thread,
In every silence, words left unsaid.
Through every sorrow, every delight,
We find our way, through the endless night.

Hands Held Tight

Fingers entwined, spirits in sync,
In this moment, we never blink.
With every heartbeat, we feel the flame,
In quiet whispers, we stake our claim.

Through storms we weather, together we stand,
With strength unyielding, hand in hand.
The world may spin, chaos may call,
But in this embrace, we conquer it all.

Memories crafted in the dark of the night,
Our souls aglow, everything feels right.
Through every challenge, through every fight,
The light of our bond shines ever bright.

In dance and in laughter, through sorrow and joy,
With you beside me, I'll never be coy.
Together we'll wander, as life's pages turn,
With hearts that ignite, like a vibrant burn.

So let time keep moving, let shadows grow long,
In your grasp, I find where I belong.
For every heartbeat, each breath, a delight,
Together we soar, hands held tight.

Luminescent Hearts

In moonlit glow, our dreams ignite,
Two luminescent hearts take flight.
Through endless skies, we chase the dawn,
In the tapestry of love, we are drawn.

Radiant moments, painted with care,
Every heartbeat sings, a truth we share.
Through shadows and light, our spirits gleam,
In the silence, we whisper our dream.

Stars whisper secrets, softly they twirl,
In this vast universe, you are my pearl.
Together we wander, where wonders unfurl,
With every adventure, our hearts gently whirl.

In gardens of hope, our laughter blooms,
Every touch felt through fragrant plumes.
With you by my side, the world is clear,
In the glow of our love, there's nothing to fear.

Forever is ours, in twilight's embrace,
With luminescent hearts, we'll find our place.
In the universe's arms, we find our start,
Two souls united, forever apart.

Strands of Affection

In the quiet weave of night's embrace,
Strands of affection, soft and laced.
Binding our hearts, a delicate thread,
In every moment, love is spread.

With gentle touches, we intertwine,
In every heartbeat, your pulse, mine.
Time may slip, like sand in hand,
But in this bond, we always stand.

Through laughter's echo and whispered sighs,
Our dreams take flight, like birds in the skies.
With every glance, every shared delight,
These strands of affection, forever ignite.

In the tapestry woven, colors collide,
With shades of our love, nothing to hide.
In every corner, with hope we sew,
Strands of affection forever will grow.

So cherish this bond, as seasons unfold,
With every heartbeat, and stories retold.
In the garden of love, let our spirits blend,
Strands of affection, with no end.

Souls Colliding

In the dance of fate we meet,
Two spirits intertwined, sweet.
Whispers echo in the night,
Hearts ablaze, a shared light.

Eyes like stars, they draw us near,
Silent promises we hold dear.
In this moment, time stands still,
As our souls bend to love's will.

Paths converge under the moon,
A symphony, a vibrant tune.
With every laugh and every sigh,
We touch the heavens, we touch the sky.

Spinning dreams within our hands,
Building castles on soft sands.
Together we craft our fate,
In this dance, it feels so great.

As the stars fall from above,
We bathe in the light of love.
Two souls colliding, pure and free,
In this moment, just you and me.

Tapestry of Feelings

Threads of joy weave through the night,
Colors blending, a vibrant sight.
Each emotion, a stroke of grace,
Painting life in time and space.

Soft whispers in morning's breath,
Carving paths that dance with depth.
Laughter stitched in heart's embrace,
A tapestry time can't erase.

Sorrow's shade adds depth and hue,
Binding us, me and you.
Every tear, a pattern formed,
In this fabric, love is warmed.

Hope's bright thread leads us along,
A melody, a sweet song.
Together we create anew,
Our feelings spun like morning dew.

In every pattern, truth reveals,
A story told through how it feels.
Our hearts weave tightly, never part,
A living tapestry, one shared heart.

Beyond the Veil

Whispers swirl in twilight's glow,
Secrets dance, and spirits flow.
Beyond the veil, where shadows play,
Lies a world where dreams can stay.

Gossamer threads of light and shade,
Guide us through the paths we've made.
Each heartbeat draws us closer still,
In this realm, we find our will.

Time unravels, shifts and bends,
In this place, the journey never ends.
With every step, we come alive,
In the silence, souls revive.

Echoes linger, soft and sweet,
In dreams where heart and spirit meet.
Beyond the veil, love's eternal song,
In this space, we both belong.

So may we wander, hand in hand,
In this ethereal, timeless land.
Beyond the veil, our truth revealed,
In whispered secrets, our fate sealed.

Cherished Moments

In the quiet of dawn's soft light,
We gather memories, a precious sight.
Each moment holds a piece of bliss,
In gentle smiles and tender kiss.

Laughter echoes through the air,
In these seconds, love laid bare.
With each heartbeat, time stands still,
In cherished moments, hearts fulfill.

Sunset paints the world in gold,
Stories shared, both new and old.
Every glance, a spark ignites,
In our hearts, a love that lights.

As seasons change, we hold them fast,
In our minds, these moments last.
With open arms, we embrace the now,
Cherishing each breath, each vow.

In the tapestry of life we weave,
Cherished moments never leave.
Together we build, together we grow,
In every moment, love will flow.

Love's Sanctuary

In the hush of twilight glow,
Two hearts entwined, soft and slow.
Whispers shared beneath the stars,
Wrapped in dreams, free from scars.

A gentle touch, a knowing smile,
We wander here, side by side a while.
Love's embrace, our sacred space,
Time stands still in this warm place.

With every breath, our spirits soar,
In this haven, we explore.
Infinite moments, pure and bright,
In love's sanctuary, our light.

Together we weave, our souls aligned,
In this refuge, our hearts designed.
Every heartbeat, a promise made,
In love's warm arms, we won't fade.

As shadows dance on evening's tide,
In this safe haven, we confide.
Through storms and trials, we will stand,
In love's sanctuary, hand in hand.

Mosaic of Us

Fragments of laughter, pieces of tears,
Each memory crafted through the years.
Colors collide in vibrant array,
A tapestry where we both stay.

Moments like pearls strung on a thread,
In every space, the words we said.
Building a world where dreams unfold,
In every heartbeat, stories told.

A collage of dreams, both big and small,
Together we rise, never to fall.
In every shadow, light will break,
A mosaic formed, for our hearts' sake.

Each piece fits in a perfect place,
Together we find our unique grace.
An artful journey, forever true,
In this mosaic, it's me and you.

The beauty lies in what we create,
In every choice, in every fate.
A masterpiece forged from love's design,
In this mosaic, your heart is mine.

Heartfelt Echoes

In the quiet moments, whispers remain,
Echoes of laughter, shadows of pain.
Each heartbeat tells stories of old,
A rhythm of love, both tender and bold.

Feelings like ripples across mirrored streams,
Reflecting the hopes and the softest dreams.
In the depths of silence, truths unfold,
Heartfelt echoes, a treasure to hold.

Through every challenge, we rise and bend,
In the space between, our hearts defend.
Each echo a promise, a vow to keep,
In the lull of the night, we softly weep.

The past intertwines with the paths we tread,
In heartfelt echoes, love's thread is spread.
A song of devotion that never will part,
In the echoes of time, you dwell in my heart.

As seasons change and moments pass by,
Together we soar, reaching for the sky.
Each echo a chorus, forever it sings,
In the dance of our love, the joy it brings.

Sails of Emotion

With winds of hope, we raise the sails,
Navigating through life's gales.
Each wave a challenge, each gust a guide,
On the seas of emotion, we turn with pride.

The tides of laughter, pull us near,
In the storms of doubt, I won't fear.
Together we journey, hearts as one,
Under the glow of the warming sun.

With every swell, our spirits dance,
In this tender voyage, we take a chance.
Through calm and chaos, we will prevail,
With love as our anchor, we'll set our sail.

The horizon beckons, our dreams in sight,
Navigating through the starry night.
With sails of emotion, we'll chart our way,
In the ocean of life, come what may.

As we traverse this vast expanse,
In the rhythm of waves, we find our chance.
Together we'll sail, through joy and strife,
With sails of emotion, we embrace life.

Elysian Echoes

In shadows soft, where whispers call,
The echoes dance, a gentle thrall.
Beneath the stars, a timeless flow,
In the night's embrace, we come to know.

With every breath, a memory gleams,
Of distant lands and woven dreams.
The heartbeats blend, a symphony,
In Elysian light, forever free.

In misty realms where spirits play,
The echoes guide us, lead the way.
With open arms, the night unfolds,
A tapestry of stories told.

Through mist and star, the journey spins,
With laughter bright, the soul begins.
In every sigh, a promise shared,
Through Elysian echoes, we are bared.

Upon the breeze, sweet tunes arise,
A language spoken through our eyes.
In sacred space, we find our peace,
From echoes soft, our hearts release.

The Caress of Understanding

In quiet moments, true hearts meet,
A gentle touch, a loving beat.
With every glance, the world dissolves,
In the caress, our doubt resolves.

Words unspoken, the heart knows well,
In silence deep, our souls do dwell.
A spark ignites, a fiery thread,
With every heartbeat, love is fed.

Through storms we stand, a steadfast pair,
In every struggle, we lay bare.
An open mind, an open heart,
In understanding, we shall not part.

In shared laughter, warmth ignites,
Through tender glances, all feels right.
Each gentle sigh, a sacred bond,
In the caress, we rise beyond.

The world may shift, but here we stay,
In the light of love, we find our way.
Through every trial, we rise and learn,
In the caress of trust, we yearn.

Enchanted Souls

Two wandering hearts in twilight's glow,
In enchanted realms where soft winds blow.
Through meadows bright, we dance in time,
Lost in the rhythm, a gentle rhyme.

In moonlit nights, our wishes soar,
A tapestry woven, forevermore.
With every step, the stardust swirls,
In this fairy tale, our magic twirls.

Beyond the veil, where dreams reside,
In harmony, the worlds collide.
With whispered secrets, we paint the air,
In enchanted souls, we weave our care.

Through evergreen forests and sapphire seas,
In loving echoes, we find our peace.
With open hearts, the journey calls,
In enchanted souls, we break down walls.

Together we soar, over hills and glades,
In the light of dawn, our love cascades.
With every twist, our spirits blend,
Enchanted souls, on love we depend.

From Roots to Wings

In autumn's grace, the leaves fall down,
A tapestry rich, nature's crown.
From roots we grow, entwined and strong,
In every heartbeat, we belong.

Through winter's chill, we stand our ground,
In silent strength, our love is found.
With each new dawn, the sun will rise,
From roots to wings, we touch the skies.

In springtime blooms, the world awakes,
With colors bright, our journey shakes.
Through summer's warmth, our spirits lift,
From roots to wings, love is our gift.

With every challenge, we rise anew,
In shared endeavors, the bond is true.
Through life's vast sea, we sail and sing,
Together we rise, from roots to wings.

In every moment, we intertwine,
In love's embrace, our hearts align.
From grounded depths, to heights we fling,
In this dance of life, our spirits cling.

Eternal Kindred

In twilight's glow, we find our path,
Two souls wandering, free from wrath.
Through echoes of time, our hearts reside,
In whispers soft, no need to hide.

Beneath the stars, we share our dreams,
Every moment, woven like streams.
In the silence, our love ignites,
A bond unbroken, through day and nights.

With every breath, I feel you near,
A sacred bond, no space for fear.
We dance in shadows, our spirits soar,
Connected forever, I want no more.

The world may change, but we remain,
In laughter, sadness, joy, and pain.
Our hearts, a canvas, painted bright,
Two kindred souls, in love's pure light.

And as the seasons fade away,
Our love endures, come what may.
In every heartbeat, I'll stand tall,
Eternal kindred, we have it all.

Heartstrings Entwined

Each laugh we share, a gentle thread,
In this vast tapestry, we are led.
Like notes in song, our voices blend,
On heartstrings taut, where dreams ascend.

Through storms and calm, we navigate,
Together we rise, never too late.
In every glance, a secret vow,
Two souls entwined, here and now.

Your heartbeats echo, a soothing balm,
In chaos found, we are the calm.
With hands held tight, we face the night,
Through shadows deep, we find the light.

These heartstrings, stretched, yet never break,
In every moment, love's soft quake.
A melody played, so sweet and true,
As long as I breathe, I'll cherish you.

So let the world spin on its axis,
Together we thrive, amid the praxis.
A tapestry woven, forever combined,
In this life, our heartstrings twined.

Whispered Promises

In twilight hush, your voice I hear,
Softly spoken, always near.
Whispers float on evening air,
Promises linger, a tender stare.

With every word, a soft caress,
In dreams we weave, a gentle mess.
Through time and space, our vows unfold,
Stories cherished, love retold.

Underneath a blanket of stars,
We share the secrets, healing scars.
A sacred trust, a bond so true,
In whispered tones, I find you.

The night wraps round, a sweet embrace,
In every heartbeat, your gentle face.
Together we rise, the dawn in sight,
With whispered promises, love ignites.

So let the world echo our song,
In whispered dreams, where we belong.
Forevermore, I'll pledge to you,
These whispered promises, ever new.

Embrace of Souls

In the quiet night, our spirits meet,
In the embrace of souls, oh so sweet.
With open hearts, we gently sway,
In timeless dance, come what may.

Each look exchanged, a silent vow,
In warm embrace, we live the now.
With every heartbeat, whispers breathe,
In sacred union, we find reprieve.

Through trials faced, hand in hand,
In every challenge, together we stand.
The world can fade, but we remain,
In this embrace, love'll never wane.

Every moment shared, a treasure rare,
In the embrace of souls, we lay bare.
With tender touches, a spark ignites,
Two wandering hearts, soaring to heights.

So let the stars weave their destiny,
In the lush embrace, we find the key.
In love's great voyage, forever whole,
In the embrace of souls, two become one.

Kindred Spirits Unveiled

In twilight's hush, we find our breath,
Two souls entwined, defying death.
With whispered dreams, we dance as one,
A bond that glows like morning sun.

Through laughter shared, and tears once shed,
We walk this path, where few have tread.
Kindred spirits, bold and free,
In the quiet, we just be.

A spark ignites with every glance,
In silent moments, hearts enhance.
No need for words; we understand,
Together strong, we take our stand.

In shadows cast, our stories twine,
Each beat a rhythm, pure and divine.
With every trial, we rise anew,
Two hearts in sync, forever true.

So let the world spin fast and bright,
In our refuge, all feels right.
Unveiled by love, we find our way,
Kindred spirits, come what may.

Joy in Silenced Moments

In stillness found within the dark,
A spark ignites, a hidden mark.
With quiet breaths, the world stands still,
In profound peace, our hearts fulfill.

A gentle smile, a knowing glance,
In silenced moments, we find our dance.
No need for chatter, just be near,
In whispers soft, we feel less fear.

The morning dew, the evening light,
In every pause, we find delight.
With gratitude, we taste the air,
Joy blooms vibrant, everywhere.

As shadows play upon the ground,
In quietude, love's grace is found.
An ache for noise fades away,
In silence, joy begins to sway.

With hands entwined, we wander free,
Finding joy in simplicity.
In humbleness, our spirits rise,
In silenced moments, love never lies.

A Garden of Heartbeats

In a garden where dreams take flight,
Heartbeats bloom, a lovely sight.
Each whisper soft, a petal's kiss,
In nature's arms, we find our bliss.

The fragrance sweet, the colors bright,
In every corner speaks the light.
With roots entwined, we grow as one,
A tapestry beneath the sun.

The fluttering leaves, a gentle breeze,
In this haven, time seems to freeze.
We tend to love, with patience deep,
In every heart, our secrets keep.

As moonlight dances on the ground,
In shadows cast, our joys are found.
With each heartbeat, nature sings,
A symphony of living things.

In every flower, a story told,
Of love and courage, fierce and bold.
A garden thrives where spirits meet,
With every heartbeat, life's truly sweet.

Mirrored Reflections

In glassy pools, the world lies still,
A mirrored dance upon the hill.
With eyes that seek, we find our place,
In quiet waters, we trace their face.

Reflections tell of dreams unspoken,
With whispers fading, hearts are broken.
In the stillness, shadows creep,
Through mirrored realms, we dare to leap.

A fleeting glance, a moment caught,
In every echo, battle fought.
With silent screams, we face the truth,
In mirrored depths, we recapture youth.

As ripples fade, new visions rise,
In reflections clear, we seek the skies.
With courage bold, we dive right in,
To find the depths that lie within.

In angles sharp, and curves so sweet,
Mirrored reflections, where hearts meet.
With every glance, a story spun,
Together we shine, two beats as one.

Inner Blossoms

In silence blooms a thought,
A whisper in the mind,
Petals soft, colors bright,
Awakening, unconfined.

Within the heart, they swell,
Yearning for the light,
Roots entangled deep below,
Reaching for the heights.

Gentle breezes guide the way,
To share what's deep inside,
As each blossom tells a tale,
Of hopes and dreams and pride.

Time may pass, the seasons change,
Yet still they stand so tall,
A garden rich with inner truths,
Resilient through it all.

So nurture each small spark you find,
Let visions fully bloom,
For inner blossoms hold the key,
To dispel the darkest gloom.

Radiant Soulmates

Across the stars, two spirits roam,
With hearts that intertwine,
Each glance a spark, a soft embrace,
In love's pure, endless line.

Together through the stormy nights,
And in the golden glow,
They share their dreams, their hopes in flight,
With every ebb and flow.

From whispers sweet to laughter bright,
Their bond forever strong,
In silent moments, time stands still,
Together, they belong.

With every step upon this earth,
They dance in harmony,
Two radiant souls, one destined path,
In perfect symphony.

So hold your soulmate, cherish deep,
In twilight's soft embrace,
For in their light, you find your home,
A love time can't erase.

Secrets Beneath the Surface

Beneath the waves, the secrets sleep,
In shadows, they reside,
Whispers of the deep unknown,
In currents' gentle tide.

Stories woven, threads of truth,
Within the ocean's song,
In silence, mysteries unfold,
Where hidden dreams belong.

The depths may hide a fragile heart,
A treasure, pure and rare,
For every gentle wave that breaks,
Reveals a longing stare.

Dive deep into the hidden realms,
Where silence softly speaks,
Each secret holds a fragment lost,
The past is what one seeks.

So ponder not just on the shore,
Where glimmers catch the eye,
For secrets breathe beneath the waves,
In depths of the vast sky.

Unseen Bonds

Invisible threads tie us so close,
In moments lost in time,
A glance, a touch, a gentle breeze,
Unseen and yet divine.

Connections forged within the heart,
In laughter and in tears,
Through every high and every low,
These bonds will persevere.

An energy that flows like light,
Between two souls aligned,
A knowing glance, a silent prayer,
In union deeply twined.

Though miles may stretch and silence reign,
These ties will never break,
For love defies the vast expanse,
And keeps the bond awake.

So cherish those you hold so dear,
In every moment shared,
For unseen bonds are stronger still,
In love, we are ensnared.

A Glow in the Heart

In shadows deep, a light does spark,
A whisper soft within the dark.
It flickers bright, a gentle hue,
A warmth that flows from me to you.

Each memory glows, a cherished flame,
Binding our souls, igniting the same.
In laughter shared, in silence sweet,
A heart's embrace, where love's complete.

Through trials faced and storms endured,
This inner light shall be secured.
It guides our way, a steady hand,
A glow within, a love so grand.

So hold it close, this radiant spark,
In every dawn and evening dark.
Together, we shall light the way,
A glow in hearts, come what may.

Forever bound by this bright flame,
In dreams and hopes, we share the same.
A glow that warms, forever bright,
In every heart, love's purest light.

The Bridge of Us

Across the river, wide and deep,
A bridge is built, our souls to keep.
With every step, we grow more strong,
In harmony, we both belong.

Each wooden plank, a tale retold,
Of dreams we've shared, of hands to hold.
The echoes of our laughter ring,
The bridge of us, a sacred thing.

Through storms and trials, we shall stand,
Hand in hand, we'll face this land.
No chasm great can tear apart,
The bond we hold within our heart.

With every dawn, this bridge we tread,
In love's embrace, we forge ahead.
Together strong, we weave our fate,
On this bridge of love, we celebrate.

So let the world be wild and vast,
Our bridge will hold, it shall not cast.
In every heartbeat, love's sweet trust,
Forever stands the bridge of us.

Gardens of Trust

In the garden where dreams take root,
Where whispers grow and shadows suit.
Seeds of trust in soil so pure,
In gentle hands, we nurture sure.

With every bloom, our hearts entwined,
In fragrant air, our love defined.
Petals soft that touch the sky,
In gardens rich, our spirits fly.

The weeds may come, the storms may rage,
Yet through it all, we turn the page.
In every trial, we find the way,
In gardens of trust, love's light shall stay.

Together we'll tend this sacred space,
A haven found, a warm embrace.
With every seed, our bond shall grow,
In gardens lush, our love we sow.

So walk with me through verdant glades,
In trust we dwell, where love cascades.
Forever may our garden thrive,
In bloom and beauty, we are alive.

Near Yet Far

In moments fleeting, time can sway,
You're in my thoughts, both night and day.
Though distance stretches like a star,
In every heartbeat, near yet far.

A quiet glance across the room,
A silent wish in twilight's gloom.
In dreams, I find your spirit near,
In whispered hopes, I feel you here.

Though miles may stretch, our bond holds tight,
A tethered thread in darkest night.
In every smile, in every tear,
Our souls embrace, though you're not here.

The moon may rise, the sun may fade,
Yet love endures, it won't be stayed.
Each moment shared, a memory star,
Attests to love, though near yet far.

So hold my heart, though paths may part,
You're ever close within my heart.
And as the world spins, we won't mar,
The love that ties: near yet far.

Radiant Companionship

In laughter's embrace we reside,
Hearts intertwined, side by side.
Each moment a gem in the sea,
Together we bloom, just you and me.

Through storms we shall weather, so bold,
Writing our story, forever told.
Hand in hand, as our dreams ignite,
In the warmth of day and the glow of night.

With whispers shared under stars bright,
Every glance feels just so right.
In silence, a language we speak,
Building our future, unique and sleek.

Radiating joy, our spirits soar,
Each treasure we find, we will explore.
In the dance of life, with rhythm we sway,
Companions forever, come what may.

Together we shine like the sun's embrace,
In the tapestry of time, we find our place.
In the heart of companionship, love is true,
A bond ever radiant, me and you.

Invisible Bonds

A glance that speaks without a sound,
In hidden corners, love is found.
Threads unseen, yet oh so tight,
Weave our hearts in day and night.

A gentle smile, a knowing nod,
Paths entwined by fate's own rod.
Though miles apart, we feel so near,
In the silence, our hearts hear.

With every heartbeat, every sigh,
Invisible ties, you and I.
In moments small, our truths reside,
In every challenge, at our side.

Through winding roads, together we roam,
In the whispers of time, we find our home.
In the softest touch, a world we know,
In the dance of life, our spirits glow.

No barriers can halt this flight,
As we embrace both day and night.
In invisible bonds, love's light is spun,
Together, forever, we are one.

Warmth of Togetherness

In cozy corners, laughter rings,
Around the hearth, love gently clings.
With every shared meal, stories unfold,
In the warmth of togetherness, we are bold.

A blanket wrapped, we watch the stars,
Counting dreams, forgetting scars.
Through seasons changing, hand in hand,
In each other's arms, we take a stand.

The gentle touch, the softest sigh,
Speaking truths that never die.
In every moment, sweet delight,
In togetherness, the world feels right.

Through laughter and tears, we intertwine,
In the tapestry of love, threads divine.
With hearts aglow and spirits free,
Together's warmth is home to me.

As sunsets fade into the night,
In the glow of love, we find our light.
With every heartbeat, we stay so near,
In the warmth of togetherness, love draws near.

Castles in the Sky

We build our dreams on clouds so high,
With hope as the hammer, and stars as our tie.
In castles of wishes, we play and roam,
In imaginary worlds, we find our home.

With laughter as bricks, and passion the stone,
We shape a realm where love is sown.
Through vibrant hues, we sketch the day,
In castles in the sky, we drift and sway.

Each dream a feather, light as air,
Together we soar, without a care.
The winds of fortune guide our flight,
In castles of dreams, we find our light.

In the azure expanse, we dance and spin,
With every heartbeat, we let love win.
Through clouds of wonder, our spirits blend,
In castles in the sky, the journey won't end.

With horizons vast and futures bright,
In every star, our dreams take flight.
Together we'll build, forever we'll try,
In the realm of love, our castles in the sky.

Threads of Destiny

In the loom of time we weave,
Fate's patterns softly glow,
Each thread a choice we believe,
In moments lost and slow.

Tangled paths that twist and turn,
Guided by the heart's own fire,
With dreams that flicker, long to burn,
We chase what we desire.

Woven tight, our stories blend,
Together, strong and bright,
Through trials faced, we find a friend,
In shadows, seek the light.

The tapestry, a work of art,
Each knot tells of our pain,
Yet through the fractures, life imparts,
A beauty born of rain.

So hold the threads with gentle care,
Embrace what life bestows,
For in this dance, we learn to share,
The fate that each one knows.

The Path of Tenderness

On the road where kindness flows,
Footsteps light and true,
With every smile, a blossom grows,
In hearts, warmth breaks through.

Gentle whispers in the breeze,
Soft touches, hands that heal,
Compassion's song, a soothing tease,
That time cannot conceal.

Through shadows deep, the heart will roam,
Seeking solace, finding grace,
In every soul, we build a home,
A shared and sacred space.

Tender voices, brave and clear,
United in our quest,
We find our strength when love is near,
In vulnerability, we rest.

So walk this path with open hearts,
Let every moment shine,
For in the love that never parts,
We draw the world divine.

Radiance of Connection

In the glow of shared delight,
Hearts entwine, softly blend,
With laughter bright, like stars at night,
A bond that time won't end.

Through eyes that meet, our stories flow,
A tapestry of life,
In silence shared, emotions grow,
Two souls escape the strife.

With every word, a spark ignites,
In moments, truth unfolds,
Together weaving future sights,
In trust, the heart beholds.

The dance of souls, a gentle sway,
A rhythm soft and pure,
In every heartbeat, love will play,
In warmth, we are secure.

So cherish every path we share,
The radiance we create,
For in connection, love lays bare,
A force that conquers fate.

Binding Shadows

In the dusk where echoes blend,
Shadows whisper tales untold,
Secrets shared, as night descends,
Fears that spark, yet bold.

Bound by dreams and silent screams,
We tread the line of night,
In hidden realms, where nothing seems,
To steal away our light.

In shadows deep, the truth may hide,
Yet courage guides us through,
With every step, we feel the tide,
A shift to something new.

Embrace the dark, let it enfold,
For in the night, we find,
A strength within, a heart of gold,
Our paths forever twined.

So walk with me, through shadows cast,
Together we will stand,
In binding twilight, shadows last,
With courage, hand in hand.

Journey to Us

Through winding roads we tread,
With dreams held close like thread.
Each step a tale, a whispered sigh,
Together we reach for the vast sky.

The stars align with every turn,
In our hearts, a fire will burn.
Hand in hand, we face the night,
Guided by love's steadfast light.

Mountains rise, yet we climb high,
Chasing sunsets, just you and I.
With every mile, our story grows,
In the depths, our spirit flows.

Echoes of laughter fill the air,
In the silence, we are a prayer.
Every journey has its mark,
But ours is defined by the spark.

So let's walk beyond the dawn,
With hope renewed, we carry on.
Each moment shared, a precious gift,
In this journey, our souls uplift.

Kisses in the Dark

In shadows we find our place,
Soft whispers touch, a warm embrace.
Each kiss ignites the starlit night,
In this realm, everything feels right.

Fingers intertwined, hearts aligned,
Lost in the moment, perfectly blind.
The world outside fades away,
In silence, words can nobly sway.

Every brush is a gentle spark,
In the quiet, we leave a mark.
Embracing dreams, hidden from sight,
Kisses bloom in the velvet night.

With each heartbeat, secrets unfold,
In the dark, our story is told.
These moments crafted, pure and fraught,
In the stillness, love is sought.

So let's linger, just you and me,
In this dance of mystery.
Wrapped in shadows, we softly part,
Leaving echoes of love in the dark.

Enchanted Connections

Beneath the moonlight's gentle grace,
Our spirits dance in a tender space.
With glances that weave through the night,
New worlds awaken, filled with light.

Magic flows in the words we share,
A bond unbroken, beyond compare.
In each heartbeat, a rhythm starts,
Two souls entwined, two beating hearts.

Whispers of fate lead us to see,
The beauty in you, the magic in me.
With every touch, enchantment grows,
In these connections, true love flows.

Moments captured in timeless frames,
In laughter and joy, we learn our names.
Together we carve our own story,
In the light of love, we find our glory.

So let the stars be our witness dear,
In this journey, there's nothing to fear.
With enchanting ties that never sever,
Together forever, always and ever.

Unbreakable Bonds

Through storms that rage and skies that cry,
Our bonds endure, we'll never die.
In the silence, strength is found,
Together in love, forever bound.

When shadows loom and doubts arise,
We face them strong with unwavering eyes.
Like roots that cling to the sturdy earth,
Unbreakable bonds bring us rebirth.

In laughter shared and tears embraced,
Every moment holds a sacred place.
With trust that flourishes and colors bright,
We navigate through day and night.

No distance can break the ties we weave,
In every word, we choose to believe.
Through thick and thin, we'll surely stand,
Together, united, hand in hand.

So here we are, through time and space,
A testament of love's true grace.
In every heartbeat, a promise made,
Unbreakable bonds that will never fade.

The Language of Us

In whispers soft, we share our dreams,
Through laughter bright, or so it seems.
Our hearts unfold, like petals bloom,
In every glance, we find our tune.

Your gaze, a map of roads unknown,
In silence deep, a bond has grown.
We speak in sighs, in every breath,
A tapestry of life and death.

With every touch, we weave the tale,
Of love's embrace, we cannot fail.
In shadows cast, our secrets lie,
Together here, we touch the sky.

Through storms we stand, we brave the night,
In darkest hours, we find the light.
Our voices merge in harmony,
The language spoken, you and me.

As time rolls on, our spirits bind,
In memories held, our paths aligned.
With every word, an echo flows,
In the language of us, love grows.

Threads of Eternity

In twilight's glow, we stitch our fate,
With threads of gold, we hesitate.
Each moment spun, a fragile weave,
In patterns bold, we dare believe.

The loom of time, it gently turns,
As life unfolds, our passion burns.
With every strand, a story told,
In fibers strong, our dreams unfold.

Through joy and sorrow, we create,
A fabric rich, we celebrate.
Intertwined, our souls belong,
In harmony, we weave our song.

In silence shared, the world grows vast,
With laughter's thread, we hold it fast.
A tapestry of moments fine,
In threads of eternity, you are mine.

The needle dances, swift and sure,
In every stitch, our love endures.
Through seasons change, our colors blend,
Two hearts entwined, it will not end.

The Fire Within

A flicker glows beneath the skin,
A hidden spark, the fire within.
In shadows cast, it softly glints,
With every breath, my spirit hints.

Through trials faced, we stoke the flame,
In quiet strength, we breathe your name.
Resilience forged in hot embrace,
With every trial, we find our place.

In passions bright, our souls ignite,
With fervent hope, we chase the light.
The warmth of love, a guiding star,
It leads us close, no matter how far.

Through winds that howl and storms that rage,
We stand as one, we turn the page.
With every tear, a new spark flies,
The fire within, it never dies.

In darkest times, we light the way,
With hearts ablaze, we greet the day.
Together forged, in flames we sing,
The fire within, our offering.

Distant Horizons

The dawn appears on distant shores,
A canvas stretched, the ocean soars.
With every wave, a whisper calls,
In every breath, the vastness sprawls.

The sky alights in hues of fire,
With dreams that dance, we lift them higher.
In search of lands where freedom rings,
With open arms, our spirit sings.

The mountains loom, the valleys deep,
In every heart, a promise keeps.
As sunsets blend with evening's grace,
We long to find our destined place.

Through trials faced, and journeys long,
In distant horizons, we belong.
With footsteps bold, we carve the way,
To lands anew, we find our sway.

The stars above, our guiding light,
In dreams unleashed, we take to flight.
In unity, we face the dawn,
To distant horizons, and beyond.

Milton Keynes UK
Ingram Content Group UK Ltd.
UKHW031322271124
451618UK00007B/125